Things I'd Like to Know

BEFORE WE GET

MARRIED!

©The Life Graduate Publishing Group

No part of this book may be scanned, reproduced or distributed in any printed or electronic form without the prior permission of the author or publisher.

ABOUT THE JOURNAL

Getting married is one of the most important decision that you will ever make. When you get married, you are making a life-long relationship commitment towards each other. It is therefore so important that you know many of the things that may never have been asked!

This journal has been split into 3 sections:

Section 1: Partner 1 Story and Answers
Section 2: Partner 2 Story and Answers
Section 3: Your Journey Together

ABOUT THE COUPLE

Place Your Photo here

Partner 1
Name: _______________________________

Partner 2
Name:_______________________________

Wedding Date - if known _______________

Signature   Signature

Partner 1   **Partner 2**

BEFORE WE GET MARRIED!

SECTION 1 - PARTNER 1

It's time to answer your questions!

Just the Basics! 

Full Name at Birth

____

Date of Birth   /   /

Time of Birth   :

Day of the week you were born?

Height at birth?

Weight at birth?

Place of Birth (City/Town and Country)

____

Hospital Name or Location of Birth

____

____

Baby talk...

What have you been told about you as a baby?

Share with me some information about your parents?

Did you have any unique characteristics or funny things you did as a baby?

Baby talk continued..

What were your first words?

____

Were you in good health as a baby?

____

____

Do you have any other baby memories to share?

____

____

____

____

____

____

____

The Young Years

What are your fondest memories growing up between the ages of 5 years to 12 years?

The Young Years Continued...

Where did you grow up as a child?
(House,location, town etc)

Who was your best friend or your best friends as a kid?

What was your favorite day of the week and why?

The Young Years Continued...

What did you want to be when you were a child?

____

What elementary/primary school did you go to and where was it located?

____

____

Describe your most memorable moment or story from school.

____

____

____

____

____

____

____

____

The Young Years Continued...

What was your favorite toy growing up?

____

____

Did you have a pet or any pets?

____

____

What was your favorite T.V show to watch as a kid?

____

____

Was there a moment you remember getting into big trouble as a child? Was there a punishment?

____

____

____

____

____

Teenage Years

What high school did you attend and where was it located?

Who was you favorite teacher or coach and why?

What was your favorite subject at school?

Did you date anyone at high school?

Teenage Years

Describe your dress sense and clothing as a teenager. Is there anything that stands out for you?

____

____

____

When and where did you learn to drive a vehicle?

____

____

What was your first vehicle and how much did you purchase it for? Tell me your best learner driving story!

____

____

____

____

____

____

Teenage Years

What hobbies did you have as a teenager?

What is your most memorable moment as a teenager?

If you knew what you know today, what would you have done differently as a teenager?

Teenage Years

Who was in your friendship group in your late teens?

____

____

____

____

Did you have any nicknames?

____

____

What 5 words come to mind to describe your teenage years?

1. ____

2. ____

3. ____

4. ____

5. ____

When I was....

When I was a teenager, I had a crush on.....

When I was in my final year of Elementary/Primary School, I was perhaps best known for....

When I was 12 yrs old, I wanted to be a......

When I was 17 years old, my favorite music and band was..

When I was in 18, the thing I wish I had more than anything else was...

When I was young, I loved to travel to.......

When I was....

When I was 18 yrs, I had a reputation for....

____

____

When I was in my teens, the biggest news story that stands out to me was.....

____

____

____

When I was growing up, the 3 favorite movies I remember watching were:

1. ____

2. ____

3. ____

My Family History

My grandparents names were:

Grandmother:

Grandfather:

They were born in: (country)
Grandmother:

Grandfather:

This is something that not many people may know about my family....

Additional Family History information:

GrandFather

GrandFather

Grandmother

Grandmother

Mother

Father

Me

Deep & Meaningful

I wish I had the opportunity to...

____

____

____

The quote that resonates most with me is..

____

____

____

My favorite book of all time is:

____

If there is one thing I would like to be known for, it would be:

____

____

____

Deep & Meaningful

Not many people know this about me, so let me share it with you:

____

____

____

____

____

____

____

The activity or hobby that I enjoy most to do now is.....

____

____

I have the unique ability to be able to....

____

____

____

Deep & Meaningful

If I was able to go back to a special time in my life, it would be...

___

If I was to pass on one word of advice to others, it would be..

___

There are special moments in life that you wish you could pause to enjoy for longer. Mine would be......

___

When I look back on my life so far, my 3 proudest moments are:

1

2

3

If there were 3 famous people that I could have dinner with, they would be:

1

2

3

Employment

From my teen years, these are the jobs/employment that
I've had:

The most enjoyable job I've had so far has been....

I think you need to know this! 

My thoughts on having a family together...

____

____

____

When it comes to money and finances, I think we should ensure that.....

____

____

____

If I could describe my perfect home, it would look like this.....

____

____

____

These are the qualities that I saw in you that confirmed that I wanted to spend the rest of my life with you.

____

____

____

____

I think you need to know this!

When I am 60 years, I would love to be living....

If you were to take me somewhere special, it would be...

My perfect day with you would look like this....

Intimacy and romance - This is what they mean to me...

If I was given $10,000 right now, I would........

The most interesting place I have ever traveled too has been.... (include the year/date this occurred)

If I was given a free return flight to anywhere in the world, I would visit...(include your 'Why')

The final word..

There have been many questions that I have answered in this journal, but I would also like to share this with you as my future partner....

Your time to write anything else you wish to share

Notes

Notes

Things I'd Like to Know
BEFORE WE GET
MARRIED!

BEFORE WE GET MARRIED!

SECTION 2 - PARTNER 2

It's time to answer your questions!

Just the Basics!

Full Name at Birth

____

Date of Birth   /   /

Time of Birth   :

Day of the week you were born?

Height at birth?

Weight at birth?

Place of Birth (City/Town and Country)

____

Hospital Name or Location of Birth

____

Baby talk...

What have you been told about you as a baby?

____

____

____

____

____

Share with me some information about your parents?

____

____

____

Did you have any unique characteristics or funny things
you did as a baby?

____

____

____

Baby talk continued..

What were your first words?

____

Were you in good health as a baby?

____

____

Do you have any other baby memories to share?

____

____

____

____

____

____

____

The Young Years

What are your fondest memories growing up between
the ages of 5 years to 12 years?

The Young Years Continued...

What did you want to be when you were a child?

____

What elementary/primary school did you go to and where was it located?

____

____

Describe your most memorable moment or story from school.

____

____

____

____

____

____

____

____

Where did you grow up as a child?
(House,location, town etc)

____

____

____

____

Who was your best friend or your best friends as a kid?

____

____

What was your favorite day of the week and why?

____

____

____

____

What was your favorite toy growing up?

____

____

Did you have a pet or any pets?

____

____

What was your favorite T.V show to watch as a kid?

____

____

Was there a moment you remember getting into big trouble as a child? Was there a punishment?

____

____

____

____

____

Teenage Years

What high school did you attend and where was it located?

____

____

____

Who was you favorite teacher or coach and why?

____

____

____

What was your favorite subject at school?

____

____

Did you date anyone at high school?

____

____

____

Teenage Years

What hobbies did you have as a teenager?

____

____

What is your most memorable moment as a teenager?

____

____

____

____

____

If you knew what you know today, what would you have done differently as a teenager?

____

____

____

____

Describe your dress sense and clothing as a teenager. Is there anything that stands out for you?

When and where did you learn to drive a vehicle?

What was your first vehicle and how much did you purchase it for? Tell me your best learner driving story!

Teenage Years

Who was in your friendship group in your late teens?

____

____

____

____

Did you have any nicknames?

____

____

What 5 words come to mind to describe your teenage years?

1. _____________________________________

2. _____________________________________

3. _____________________________________

4. _____________________________________

5. _____________________________________

My Family History

My grandparents names were:

Grandmother:

Grandfather:

They were born in: (country)
Grandmother:

Grandfather:

This is something that not many people may know about my family....

Additional Family History information:

My FAMILY TREE

GrandFather

GrandFather

Grandmother

Grandmother

Mother

Father

Me

Deep & Meaningful

I wish I had the opportunity to...

____

____

____

The quote that resonates most with me is..

____

____

____

____

My favorite book of all time is:

____

If there is one thing I would like to be known for, it would be:

____

____

____

If I was able to go back to a special time in my life, it would be...

If I was to pass on one word of advice to others, it would be..

There are special moments in life that you wish you could pause to enjoy for longer. Mine would be......

Deep & Meaningful

Not many people know this about me, so let me share it with you:

____

____

____

____

____

____

____

The activity or hobby that I enjoy most to do now is.....

____

____

I have the unique ability to be able to....

____

____

____

Deep & Meaningful

When I look back on my life so far, my 3 proudest moments are:

1

2

3

If there were 3 famous people that I could have dinner with, they would be:

1

2

3

Employment

From my teen years, these are the jobs/employment that I've had:

____

____

____

____

____

____

____

The most enjoyable job I've had so far has been....

____

____

My thoughts on having a family together...

____

____

____

When it comes to money and finances, I think we should
ensure that.....

____

____

____

If I could describe my perfect home, it would look like
this.....

____

____

____

These are the qualities that I saw in you that confirmed
that I wanted to spend the rest of my life with you.

____

____

____

____

____

I think you need to know this!

When I am 60 years, I would love to be living....

If you were to take me somewhere special, it would be...

My perfect day with you would look like this....

Intimacy and romance - This is what they mean to me...

If I was given $10,000 right now, I would........

The most interesting place I have ever traveled too has been.... (include the year/date this occurred)

If I was given a free return flight to anywhere in the world, I would visit...(include your 'Why')

The final word..

There have been many questions that I have answered in this journal, but I would also like to share this with you as my future partner....

Your time to write anything else you wish to share

____

____

____

____

____

____

____

____

____

____

Notes

Notes

Things I'd Like to Know
BEFORE WE
GET
MARRIED!

SECTION 3

OUR JOURNEY TOGETHER

Add information in this section about your journey so far as a couple.

We first met at: (Location/date)

____

____

The first time we kissed was:

____

____

____

Our first real travel adventure together was:

____

____

____

____

For our honeymoon, we are planning on....

____

____

____

____

Things I'd Like to Know

BEFORE WE
GET
MARRIED!

Our Journey

Photos, moments....anything

Photos, moments....anything

Our Journey

Photos, moments....anything

Our Journey

Photos, moments....anything

Our Journey

Photos, moments....anything

Our Journey

Photos, moments....anything

Notes

Notes

BEFORE WE GET MARRIED!